Understanding Marriage God's Way

by Connie Woods

Contents

Introduction..4

Marriage Principles 6

Why Is Marriage Important Anyway? 7

7 Foundation Principles of Marriage 12

Other Practical Benefits of Marriage 39

Cleave, Love & Respect 42

Other Marriage Tips 53

Bonus: 12 Principles of Handling Conflict ...61

Plus Bonus: Understanding the Stages of

Marriage..102

Closing Remarks..............................109

Introduction

Marriage was created during the creation period, in the beginning by God. From the beginning marriage was a part of God's design and plan. God revealed his will concerning marriage through his Word and set an example by the first marriage, Adam and Eve.

Marriage is a sacred covenant between a man, woman, and God and is designed to keep a married couple holy and in right standing with God through his Son Jesus Christ with the help of the Holy Spirit. It is a covenant because God blesses the marriages of those committed to following his Word and his principles in marriage.

This book will help couples understand God's rules and expectations in marriage while building their faith and assurance. This book lays out foundation principles and includes numerous tips for a great marriage. It also includes some tips on handling conflict in marriage.

Marriage is a very serious decision and commitment. Couples make a lifelong, spiritual, emotional, and physical commitment to each other before God and witnesses. They promise to love each other, forsake all others, share their lives, intimacy, interests, money, children, joys and disappointments, and whole life together, for better or worse, until death.

Marriage Principles

- One man, one woman

- The husband should leave his mother and father and cleave to his wife (companionship, intimacy)

- Monogamous (sex only between the two of them)

- Lifetime commitment

- Hierarchy (husband leading, wife following)

- Being fruitful (producing children)

- Love & Respect

Marriage is the basic foundation of society, instituted and created by God. Marriage is a holy covenant, not a secular contract, before God. It is considered valid by God, who created it, only according as he outlined. Society is a more healthy society with marriage. When couples obey God it benefits men, women, and children.

Marriage should not be self-serving, but sacrificial, in that each person are to serve the other, centered on pleasing God, as Christ does his bride, the church.

Enduring marriages, last when there are commitments made by the husband and wife, to get through the good times and the tough times together, through Christ, in which all things are possible.

So Why is Marriage Important Anyway?

Throughout history marriage has always been defined as being between one man and one woman. Marriage was supernaturally created by God to be a basis for society, order, stability, procreation, and security.

Since God created marriage, he has the authority and right to set the rules for marriage, not men or women. Marriage has always occurred when there was a formal marriage ceremony between one man and one woman, followed with marriage being consummated with sexual intercourse, and God considered the two to become one flesh.

Whenever civilizations defiled marriage, and brought in sexual practices that were not in the confines of marriage as one man and one woman, as God ordained, that society eventually destroyed itself, or worse, God destroyed them, as in the case of Sodom & Gomorrah.

Marriage is not based on love, sexual attraction, or equality as homosexuals have argued, that have advanced their agenda; but marriage is based on God's word, one man, one woman, in a monogamous relationship, committed for life, with a hierarchy, the husband being the head, and the wife submitting (Eph.5:22) to her husband, as the husband is submitted to Christ, having the agape kind of love. Marriage must be right in God's eyes

because we live to please God and live holy.

7 Foundation Principles of Marriage

1. Marriage was Created & Designed by God

Matthew 19:5

And said, For this cause shall a man leave father and mother, and shall cleave to his wife: and they twain shall be one flesh?

[6] Wherefore they are no more twain, but one flesh. What therefore God hath joined together, let not man put asunder.

Proverbs 18:22 ESV

He who finds a wife finds a good thing and obtains favor from the Lord.

Genesis 2:18-25

And the Lord God said, It is not good that the man

should be alone; I will make him an help meet for him.

19 And out of the ground the Lord God formed every beast of the field, and every fowl of the air; and brought them unto Adam to see what he would call them: and whatsoever Adam called every living creature, that was the name thereof.

20 And Adam gave names to all cattle, and to the fowl of the air, and to every beast of the field; but for Adam there was not found an help meet for him.

21 And the Lord God caused a deep sleep to fall upon Adam, and he slept: and he took one of his ribs, and closed up the flesh instead thereof;

22 And the rib, which the Lord God had taken from man, made he a woman, and brought her unto the man.

23 And Adam said, This is now bone of my bones, and flesh of my flesh: she shall be called Woman, because she was taken out of Man.

24 Therefore shall a man leave his father and his mother, and shall cleave unto his wife: and they shall be one flesh.

25 And they were both naked, the man and his wife, and were not ashamed.

Marriage was created by God. Since God is the designer of marriage, He alone has the right to make the rules for marriage. Man has no right to change the purpose and rules of what God has set, for his own personal agenda.

There is no society that ever existed that did not have marriage. Why, because it is of spiritual origin. It was not something that man thought of or decided to have. Marriage was God's idea and plan to keep man holy and to ensure all of his needs were met; both man and woman. God loves man and in his infinite wisdom, knowledge, and understanding knows fully what man needs.

Marriage glorifies God. It depicts a picture of Christ and his bride, the church, and pleases God.

2. God Wanted Adam to have a Companion: It is Not Good for Man to Be Alone (Genesis 2:18)

Genesis 2:18-23 KJV

And the Lord God said, It is not good that the man should be alone; I will make him an help meet for him. 20 And Adam gave names to all cattle, and to the fowl of the air, and to every beast of the field; but for Adam there was not found an help meet for him. 21 And the Lord God caused a deep sleep to fall upon Adam, and he slept: and he took one of his ribs, and closed up the flesh instead thereof; 22 And the rib, which the Lord God had taken from man, made he a woman, and brought her unto the man. 23 And Adam said, This is now bone of my bones, and flesh of my flesh: she

shall be called Woman, because she was taken

out of Man.

1 Peter 3:7 ESV

Likewise, husbands, live with your wives in an

understanding way, showing honor to the woman

as the weaker vessel, since they are heirs with

you of the grace of life, so that your prayers may

not be hindered.

Genesis 1:27

"God created man in His own image, in the image

of God He created him; male and female He

created them."

Adam named all of the animals, before he was

put into a deep sleep, and God took a rib out of Adam's body, and formed Eve. Could it have been as Adam named all of the animals, male and female, Adam realized there was no female for him. After God made Eve, Adam must have been blown away with joy because of his statement, "this is now bone of my bones, and flesh of my flesh, she shall be called Woman, because she was taken out of Man". Eve would be a helper to Adam, the missing part that Adam needed and complemented him. She would have a different role and function but would be an equal with Adam, because she was also made in the image of God. Adam would be the head, Eve would follow and support him, but she would also walk beside him.

God made men and women to be ideal companions, fully compatible, and perfectly suited to meet each other's needs. God knew that woman complemented man.

Despite some of the problems and conflict that happen in marriage today, men and women still need each other. The marriage relationship is the most satisfying relationship outside of God.

3. Marriage is Between One Man & One Woman

God created for Adam, not another man (as in homosexuality) and not many wives, as in polygamy, but God created Eve, one woman, a helper suitable for Adam. God clearly stated, that the man would leave his father and mother, cleave to his wife, and the two, shall be one flesh. Mothers and fathers should raise their children so that one day they will eventually leave and fulfill the will that God has for their lives. To get an education, job, find a wife, or whatever plan God has for them.

Matthew 19:4

And he answered and said unto them, Have ye not read, that he which made them at the beginning made them male and female, [5] And said, For this cause shall a man leave father and mother, and shall cleave to his wife: and they twain shall be one flesh?

4. Monogamy and Exclusivity for a Lifetime

God could have made Adam many wives but he made him only one, Eve. This was the example. God only wanted him to have one wife. There were some in the scripture who did not follow this principle, and had many wives which caused lots of problems.

Marriage is meant to be a lifetime relationship until either the husband or wife dies. It is sinful to divorce, separate, or put one's husband or wife away, leaving for fornication.

Today divorce is rampant in our society. It is not

taken seriously. Although no fault divorces exist, there is always someone at fault or even both persons. All persons are accountable before God concerning their behavior in marriage and will answer to God. God will also bless those that obey him and do what he says concerning marriage.

1 Corinthians 7:39 ESV

A wife is bound to her husband as long as he lives. But if her husband dies, she is free to be married to whom she wishes, only in the Lord.

Romans 7:2 ESV

For a married woman is bound by law to her husband while he lives, but if her husband dies she is released from the law of marriage.

Matthew 19:9 ESV

And I say to you: whoever divorces his wife,

except for sexual immorality, and marries

another, commits adultery.

5a. Marriage is Honorable (Hebrews 13:4)

Hebrews 13:4

Marriage is honourable in all, and the bed undefiled: but whoremongers and adulterers God will judge.

Marriage is honorable, and God wants marriage to be treated honorably. Honorable is used in relation to the bed being undefiled. God says he will judge all those that dishonor the holiness of marriage in regards to sex, specifically whoremongers and adulterers. In other words, having sex with someone you are not married to is sinful, but sex with your own husband or wife is acceptable, honorable, and pleasing to God.

It is important that husbands and wives have boundaries in marriage, to ensure they live Godly and stay holy. Close relationships with the opposite sex, are probably not appropriate. It leads to undue temptation.

There should not be conversation or conduct with the opposite sex that dishonors the husband or wife. Adequate time and attention should be given to the spouse, above all other relationships and activities. This is honoring to God. God calls couples to make their marriages primary.

5b. Sexual Purity & Gratification of Sexual Desire: Avoids Fornication & the Bed is Undefiled (1 Cor. 7:3)

1 Corinthians 7:3

Nevertheless, to avoid fornication, let every man have his own wife, and let every woman have her own husband. [3] Let the husband render unto the wife due benevolence: and likewise also the wife unto the husband. [4] The wife hath not power of her own body, but the husband: and likewise also the husband hath not power of his own body, but the wife. [5] Defraud ye not one the other, except it be with consent for a time, that ye may give yourselves to fasting and prayer; and come together again, that Satan tempt you not for your

incontinency.

1 Corinthians 7:1-40 ESV

Now concerning the matters about which you

wrote: "It is good for a man not to have sexual

relations with a woman." But because of the

temptation to sexual immorality, each man should

have his own wife and each woman her own

husband. The husband should give to his wife her

conjugal rights, and likewise the wife to her

husband. For the wife does not have authority

over her own body, but the husband does.

Likewise the husband does not have authority

over his own body, but the wife does. Do not

deprive one another, except perhaps by

agreement for a limited time, that you may devote

yourselves to prayer; but then come together

again, so that Satan may not tempt you because

of your lack of self-control.

Sex is a gift from God. Sex is not defiled or sinful

when married, but is a source of gratification and

pleasure within marriage. God forbid men and

women to have sexual promiscuity, liaisons,

fornication, or adultery. Marriage keeps men and

women from sexual sin. It is the selfless duty of

the husband and wife to satisfy each other

sexually. This keeps from fornication and

adultery. It is a fulfilling part of marriage that God

considers pure and acceptable in marriage. If

every woman had her own husband and every

man had his own wife and only slept with that

person, there would be no illegitimate

pregnancies, sexually transmitted diseases, and

sexually exploited, used, and abused people.

6. Marriage Has a Hierarchy

Ephesians 5:22-24 ESV

Wives, submit to your own husbands, as to the Lord. For the husband is the head of the wife even as Christ is the head of the church, his body, and is himself its Savior. Now as the church submits to Christ, so also wives should submit in everything to their husbands.

Genesis 1:27

"God created man in His own image, in the image of God He created him; male and female He created them".

The husband is to be the head of the woman and

the woman is to submit to her husband. This is the order God created. The woman's role is different in function as a helper to the man, but her worth and nature is equal not inferior. The different roles that men and women have complement one another.

Women should not resent, be envious, or jealous of a man's headship role, or feel in competition with men. Men did not get the better end of the stick, as the leader, just a different role and function. With that role comes great responsibility, like the burden of providing for his family and making sure everyone's needs are met in the family. Just because God has ordered the man to lead, does not mean that women are loved any less by God or are of lesser value.

Women have their role and function also; primarily to take care of the husband, home, and children. All members jointly fit together. Men and women are both joint heirs, if both continue in good works, and are in the body of Christ. Just like a mother or father is not better than their child or of higher value, their roles are different.

7. Marriage is for Procreation & Produces Stable & Healthy Legitimate Children

Psalm 127:1-5 ESV

Unless the Lord builds the house, those who build it labor in vain. Unless the Lord watches over the city, the watchman stays awake in vain. It is in vain that you rise up early and go late to rest, eating the bread of anxious toil; for he gives to his beloved sleep. Behold, children are a heritage from the Lord, the fruit of the womb a reward. Like arrows in the hand of a warrior are the children of one's youth. Blessed is the man who fills his quiver with them! He shall not be put to shame when he speaks with his enemies in the gate.

Genesis 1:28 ESV

And God blessed them. And God said to them, "Be fruitful and multiply and fill the earth and subdue it and have dominion over the fish of the sea and over the birds of the heavens and over every living thing that moves on the earth."

One of God's rewards in marriage is children (the fruit of the womb). Although today many don't treat children like they are a blessing, but more of an inconvenience, scripture says that children are an heritage from the Lord, and blessed is the man who fills his quiver with them. We do our kids a service by raising them up in the fear and admonition of the Lord, teaching them God's word, teaching them how to obey God's word, teaching them how to pray, so that they can go to God for themselves, teaching them how to be filled with the Holy Ghost, and how to believe and trust God. Children raised this way do better in life and have some sense. They have a healthy fear of God and God keeps them. He blesses them in life and will lead and guide them in all aspects of their lives.

As a general rule, children living with both parents, do better than children living with only one. They are less likely to experience abuse, emotional or mental problems, less likely to be in gangs, use drugs, or be involved in illicit sexual behavior or criminal activity. They are also less likely to experience poverty. They are happier with both parents and don't have to split their loyalties between one parent or the other, as in separation or divorce. They also don't have to live in different homes with different families, when parents split up, and get used to having new parents. All this mess have an effect on the children, when parents refuse to do what God says and do their own thing, go after their own desires and lusts, refuse to get along with each other, and divorce, the children suffer. If you love your God and your kids try to work out your marriage.

Other Practical Benefits of Marriage

• Two can accomplish more, than one

Two together can get more accomplished, for God's glory, than one by himself.

• Marriage raises the living standard for women and children.

Women and children are often lifted out of poverty level just by being married. Responsible dads care for their children, and when they are around, not just a weekend dad, they have a more profound positive effect on their child's well-being. God also said he would give favor to men that are married.

- **Marriage offer mental wellness and longer life**.

Studies show that married couples tend to live longer. Marriage is so intertwined in the well-being of long time married couples they are so close they often operate as one.

- **Marriage offers security and protection**.

- **God hates divorce.**

God does not like divorce, in fact he says he hates divorce, although there are some instances in which he allows it.

Malachi 2:16 ESV

"For the man who does not love his wife but divorces her, says the Lord, the God of Israel, covers his garment with violence, says the Lord of

hosts. So guard yourselves in your spirit, and do not be faithless."

Malachi 2:15 ESV

Did he not make them one, with a portion of the Spirit in their union? And what was the one God seeking? Godly offspring. So guard yourselves in your spirit, and let none of you be faithless to the wife of your youth.

• **Marriage benefits women**.

Despite the women's movement, women who are in marriages do better than women who are not. Their income is increased by about 50%, they are less likely to experience violence, and suffer less illness. They also outlive single women.

Other Principles: Cleaving, Love, & Respect

Man Should Cleave To His Wife and Set Proper Boundaries

Genesis 2:24

Therefore shall a man leave his father and mother, and cleave to his wife, and they shall be one flesh.

Men should leave their mothers and fathers and cleave to their wife. They must leave the lesser relationships and cleave to their primary relationship. No other relationship should be as intimate emotionally, spiritually, or physically except for with God. The goal is to cleave to one another and not let others come between the marriage.

It is easy to develop intimate relationships with others, when a member of the opposite sex gets too close. This kind of connection with someone else other than the spouse, drains energy away from the marriage relationship and it can ultimately destroy the marriage. Intimate relationships should only be with the marriage partner, or couples are headed for trouble. This is how illicit affairs develop.

Guarding your heart is a practical concept, that should be closely adhered to. Proper boundaries have to always be a consideration.

Guard your mind. Don't let evil thoughts come to your mind. Cast those thoughts down immediately.

Certain aspects of the relationship should be shared with no one. Very personal things like sex, money, etc. should be kept private. Don't tell people your private business. Take it to God. When couples cleave to each other, there is no time for improper relationships with other people.

Wives are to Reverence and Respect Their Husbands

Ephesians 5:33

… and wife see that she reverence her husband. God wants women to respect their husband.

1 Peter 3:1 ESV

Likewise, wives, be subject to your own husbands, so that even if some do not obey the word, they may be won without a word by the conduct of their wives,

Respect is the number one thing a man needs, wants, and desires from his wife. To respect someone means to esteem, honor, show favor, or partiality. O how husbands would love to come home, if they knew they would be treated like royalty when they arrived. If they knew and believed their wives truly respected them.

A wife can show honor and respect to her husband by treating him with honor and by communicating with him in an honorable way at all times. Wives should let husbands know how they appreciate everything that they do. Show respect for his position in the family, as caretaker, head, or provider. What an awesome responsibility to have.

All wives may not feel that their husband are respectable, loving, or doing what he is supposed to be doing. Wives are still to respect their husbands for the position that God places him in and respect him because God said it. A wife should show respect to her husband, fearing God, and showing respect to his authority knowing that God will deal with her husband if he mistreats her or is not doing what he is supposed to be doing. To talk crazy to your husband is not God honoring, nor wise. It plants seed of resentment. Sara called Abraham 'lord' in showing her respect to him. Many marriages could be saved if there was proper respect and communication between the two.

Wives Should also Submit to Their Husbands (1 Peter 3:1, Eph. 5:22-24)

Submission is an act of the will, because no wife can be forced to submit to anyone, not even her own husband. Submission is hard to do when there is not trust in the relationship, nor trust in God. A wife has to trust her husband and/or God to follow her husbands' way instead of her own because he is not always right.

When a wife feels that her husband loves her and has her best interest at heart, it becomes easy for wives to submit to his authority. No one wants to be a doormat. Submission is often depicted this way. In a loving relationship, both husband and wife should feel valued and respected.

The biggest obstacle to submission for women is mistrust and men abusing their power. Women put up defenses, in order not to become a victim, dependent on a man, or put in a position where she can be easily taken advantage of. This is one of the primary reasons that women get their own careers or have secret bank accounts. If something ever happens she has a way to care for herself.

Women of faith, decide to trust God, and submit anyhow, believing that God will take care of her, despite the man's actions or circumstances.

Likewise, Husbands are to Love Their Wives

Ephesians 5:25 ESV

Husbands, love your wives, as Christ loved the church and gave himself up for her

Ephesians 5:33 ESV

However, let each one of you love his wife as himself, and let the wife see that she respects her husband.

God wants husbands to love their wives. He told

husbands to love their wives as they love their

own bodies. (Colossians 3:18-19). He warned

them against being bitter toward their wives, lest

their prayers be hindered. (1 Peter 3:7) Husbands

can show love to their wives by showing sincere,

warm, love and affection. They can also put time

aside to meet their wife's communication and

affection needs. Husbands should not tear down

their wives, but build her up and encourage her.

Husbands should verbalize their affections and

not assume that she knows how he feels about

her. These principles save and make the quality

of marriage better if practiced. These are sure fire

ways to developing more intimacy in a marriage

and can never be practiced enough.

Love and affection ranks in the top three things

that a woman needs.

Wives want husbands to tell them how much they are loved. She doesn't want to hear, "you already know that I love you because I pay the bills", or "I'm here".

Other Marriage Tips

1. Do Fun & Romantic Things Together

Doing fun and romantic things together is a great way to keep love alive in a relationship and is a source of enjoyment. If you're having a lot of fun together, there is little time left to argue and complain. Fun times together are not only fun but build up the marriage. Couples oftentimes forget to do fun things together, especially when they are super busy with children or are having a lot of conflict. Plan special outings that both enjoy on a consistent basis. Here are a few ideas:

• A romantic candle lit dinner

- Dinner at your favorite restaurant

- Day trip to your favorite romantic city

- Going to see a movie

- Visiting a beautiful hotel for one night or the weekend

- Taking a day cruise for a few hours

- Walking along the river or lake

- Taking a train ride and visiting somewhere new

- Seeing sites in a city you've always wanted to visit

- Getting together with friends or family

- Buying a timeshare and visiting new places

- Taking a cross country road trip

It is okay to incorporate your children in these activities, especially if they are really young, and babysitting may be a problem. Some couples are really great at incorporating their children in activities, and wouldn't have it any other way. Again, couples also need some time alone if only for a couple of hours to see a movie or have dinner.

Children benefit from happy mothers and fathers. They adapt well to routine, consistency, and lots of love. Couples that love each other, and are happy, contribute to the well-being of their children. It also teaches children what to look for in a mate, and how to behave appropriately, when they see mom and dad caring for each other.

2. Place Your Marriage First

• Don't neglect your marriage by putting it last,

behind everything else

• Set aside time to enjoy your spouse

• Don't get too busy on things that don't matter

• Enjoy leisure activities together

• Consider your mate when planning for anything.

• Be protective of one another

• Never criticize your spouse to others

• Never criticize your spouse in front of others

3. Keep Yourself Up

It is very positive in marriage, when husbands and wives take care of themselves and make themselves attractive for each other. The focus should not just be on the outer appearance, but neither should it go to the extreme other side, and not care for one's self at all. Try to make it as easy as possible for your husband and wife to live Godly.

Pay attention to healthy eating, exercise, fingernails, hair, clothing, and good hygiene. These little things can make a huge difference in your marriage. Some men and women are more particular than others. Know your mate!

Husbands should also look nice for their wives. Wives are not dead, they can see too. So it's important for husbands to work on their appearance.

4. Be Financially Responsible & Don't Get Overcommitted

To overcommit yourself financially is to add stress to your marriage. It is very easy to get in debt but very difficult to get out. To avoid this always stay within a budget. As a general rule, the first 10% is for God, the second 10% for savings, and 80% for living expenses. The 80% should also cover things like the movies, and other fun things.

Financial problems are the number one reason for divorce. It is the number one source for arguments among married couples. The goal would be to not get in situations that would put enormous strain on your marriage.

Bonus: 12 Principles of

Handling Conflict In Marriage

A gentle answer turns away wrath, but a harsh word stirs up anger (Proverbs 15:1).

An angry man stirs up dissension, and a hot-tempered one commits many sins (Proverbs 29:22).

The wise woman builds her house, but with her own hands the foolish one tears hers down (Proverbs 14:1).

Better to live in a desert than with a quarrelsome and ill-tempered wife (Proverbs 21:19).

Better to live on a corner of the roof than share a house with a quarrelsome wife (Proverbs 25:24).

• *Wives, be submissive to your husbands so that, if any of them do not believe the word, they may be won over without words by the behavior of their wives, when they see the purity and reverence of your lives.*

Your beauty should not come from outward adornment, such as braided hair and wearing of gold jewelry and fine clothes. Instead, it should be that of your inner self, the unfading beauty of a gentle and quiet spirit, which is of great worth in God's sight (1 Peter 3:1-4).

Husbands, in the same way be considerate as you live with your wives, and treat them with respect as the weaker partner and as heirs with you of the gracious gift of life, so that nothing will hinder your prayers (1 Peter 3:7).

12 Principles of Handling Conflict In Marriage

If two individuals are committed to Christ, they should be able to talk and come to an agreement. If they can't agree seeking God in prayer, searching God's word, and asking the Holy Spirit to give an answer is always the best starting point.

Unfortunately, even in Christian marriages there may be hot button issues that a couple can't agree on and can't even talk about without someone getting upset. This should not be.

If this is the case, this chapter deals with the very

basics of communicating when emotions are up
so that couples are able to talk and listen to each
other in a calm manner. Although God did ordain
the man to be the head does not mean he can't
listen to his wife express her feelings or vice-
versa.

Although this may be difficult, when you have a
very strong viewpoint, being able to listen to the
other person is vital to having a lasting marriage
with intimacy.

Principle 1: Agree to Work Through Issues, Differences, Disagreements, and Problems in a Godly manner and cast out those ungodly spirits that come against your marriage. Ask God, the Holy Spirit for Wisdom.

When disagreements arise, usually what's next is that communication breaks down. The devil is laughing and God gets no glory out of that. Both the husband and wife are frustrated, going in circles, debating, arguing, and even withdrawing. Instead of strongly debating the same points over and over, and judging who's right and who is wrong, each person with God's help, have to decide that they are really going to do what is necessary to resolve the problem and put their flesh under subjection.

The first step, in resolving conflict in any marriage, and ultimately improving the marriage, is for both to agree that they will work on solving their problems. Then they won't let the devil cause confusion. They must remember to take authority over the spirits that are not of God and cast them out; the ones that come against their marriage and ask the Holy Spirit to give them wisdom on how to resolve their issue or problem. They also have to walk in the fruit of the spirit (Galations 5:22; love, joy, peace, forbearance, kindness, goodness, faithfulness, gentleness and self-control). Man's wisdom is not equal to God's wisdom. He says his ways and thoughts are higher than our thoughts. Decide early on that you won't let differences be a stumbling block that hinder your marriage and that you will do whatever is necessary to make it work, to have a fulfilling, godly, satisfying, intimate marriage.

This is a general agreement both persons must come to, and they will begin to see change.

Before a couple can even begin to discuss any issues, they must both agree, that they agree on working to solve their problems. Again, all marriages have problems or issues that need to be addressed, at some point in their marriage it is what couples do in handling those problems that matter.

Couples should want to glorify God, and be an example that two persons can walk in agreement as one, even if they don't completely agree on everything.

Principle 2: Conduct: Prior to any Discussions, Agree to Actively Listen to One Another, and not talk while the other is talking.

The next step involves, couples agreeing on how they will conduct themselves, when they come together and talk. Both persons should agree that when they come together and talk about their issues and problems that they will actually listen to each other and not interrupt. They will conduct themselves like Christians. Not stay in their flesh. Not throw a tantrum and walk out or scream and yell. They will be patient, they will be kind, they will be gentle, they will show love, and exercise self-control.

They will not overtalk, but exercise active listening (discussed later in more detail). Agreeing to listen, also involves agreeing to listen without interrupting the other person, giving them time to express opinions and feelings without rushing them, and to allow them time to make their point. It involves making eye contact with that person and using body language that conveys respect and love.

They also agree that they will actually listen with intent to understand the other person, not to just criticize the others' viewpoint, or point out all the flaws.

This may be difficult to do initially, especially if you are really in the habit of battling, arguing, screaming, cutting off the other person while talking, and yelling your position in order to be heard. If either party is unwilling to agree to listen, this is where the breakdown begins.

Being a good listener is also an attitude of the heart. Although it is difficult to listen to points that you disagree with, because of your love for that person, you will put aside your own agenda, defenses, and goals to understand their viewpoint, even though you may not agree. Listening does not mean agreement, it is giving a person the opportunity to be and feel heard.

You and your partner, at this point, should be determining the rules and limits of listening to each other when together to discuss the hot button issues that need resolving. (E.g. taking turns talking and listening, not interrupting, eye contact, body language, and trying to understand why they feel the way they do, etc.)

Other Tips for Good

Conversation/Communication

• Have a positive attitude

• Be respectful and considerate

• For every negative comment, give at least one positive one

• Think of the other persons' needs and wants

• Be honest about your needs and wants

• Don't embarrass or shame

• Don't raise your voice.

• Remain calm when discussing heavy topics

Principle 3: Determine What the Issues and Problems Are that Create Constant Disagreement, and Establish a Good Time to Talk With No Distractions.

Set aside some alone time to discuss the issues. This time should be distraction free, from children, cell phones, television, etc. It should also be at a time that allows adequate time to thoroughly go over issues without feeling rushed. Please put all cell phones and devices away and give your husband or wife your full attention.

Each person should state what the issues are and

together agree, which one they'll tackle first. Prior ground rules on communication should already have been already set up by this point. (E.g. both agreeing to listen, no interrupting while talking, etc.)

Principle 4: When Discussing Issues Set a Time Limit on How Long Each Person Speaks With No Interruptions.

Now that issues are actually being discussed, there must be time limits so that each person can have adequate amounts of time to express their opinions and feelings. Initially, you may have to set a time limit (with a clock) of one to two minutes, so that each person can get acclimated to how long they should be talking at one time, before the other person gets his/her chance to express their feelings. Each person should have about the same amount of time to express their opinion. No person, is to be interrupted.

If a couple has a habit of over talking, cutting off, arguing, etc. they definitely need to use timed talking.

Principle 5: Communicating Effectively: Effective & Assertive Communication

To effectively communicate, one must be able to listen, be respectful, use assertive statements, and understand the other person.

Active Listening: Active Listening is not just hearing what the other person said, but being interested in what they said, with an appropriate response, showing concern, and asking more questions to fully understand.

For example: A woman states to her husband, "One of the customers, left without paying today, and I came up short on my register, so the boss yelled at me"!

A response that criticizes, or give advice may not be a good one at this point.

A more appropriate response may be. Are you feeling okay? What happened? This response shows interest, concern, appropriately responds, and seeks to fully understand their partner.

• Listening also involves repeating back what you heard, in your own words, so that your partner knows that you heard them.

Wrong response- "Your boss had good reason to yell at you, since you let the customer leave without paying. Next time watch your customers and the register!"

A more appropriate response would be - "I'm sorry, that you get yelled at by your boss, because your customer left without paying, would you like to share what happened?"

Be respectful, and avoid speaking negatively, criticizing, belittling, being sarcastic, or playing the victim. All of these are distractors from the real issue of the actual problem that you are trying to solve. It shifts the focus from solving the problem to tending to emotions that are sometimes rooted in manipulation.

It is helpful to use "I" statements, instead of blaming others or playing the victim, (i.e. "I feel", "I think", etc.). "I" statements are more assertive statements that can be used, by replacing negative statements.

Try: "When _____ happens, I

feel_____. I would like_____".

Instead of saying: Say:

You don't love me.   I feel sad when you don't

spend time with me.

You're wrong.   When you keep all the

money, I feel left out.

You make me sick.   I feel angry when you

raise your voice.

If there is a genuine difference in what both

partners want, they may have to negotiate a

solution. One partner offers the other, something

that they want, and they in return offer something

that is wanted. Keep in mind, that we do

everything to please God. The decisions that we

make must be pleasing to God, as well as

pleasing to ourselves and our spouse.

Communication Styles

There are four popular communication styles that are often used today:

Aggressive Communication. Aggressive communication doesn't care about the rights of others. It manipulates others by intimidation, attempting to make people do something, by being hostile, rude, threatening, angry, or using other negative behaviors or by laying guilt trips on people.

Passive Communication. Passive communication doesn't rock the boat, and easily gives in to others wants and desires. It won't express its own needs. It has a difficult time telling others no and setting proper boundaries, so it accepts a lot of tasks that it really doesn't want to do. It avoids confrontation at all costs, to its own expense.

Passive-Aggressive Communication. Passive aggressive makes people think you are on board but secretly resents it and won't comply. Won't tell a person how you honestly feel, but will say yes, but will not follow through or will try to derail something altogether. It is passive, and aggressive secretly.

Assertive Communication. Assertive communication is a healthy form of communication. It is honest about feelings and won't be pushed past personal limits. It respects self while respecting others. It will communicate

its own needs as well as try to find a mutual

agreement and meet others' needs.

Assertiveness is the style that most people use

the least.

Which communication style do you use the most?

Principle 6: Statement of Problem. Correctly Defining the Problem by Clarification

Sometimes problems are not what they seem. Until you have thoroughly discussed the issues, and the underlying feelings, and motives behind actions, then you can fully understand what the problem really is.

It is crucial to really clarify and define what problem needs to be solved, instead of fixing something that don't need fixing.

For example: A wife complained that her husband didn't give her enough money, and that he didn't love her anymore. The husband paid all the bills and occasionally gave his wife money of the little bit that was left after bills. He wanted to have something saved in case of an emergency, especially since he had bad credit.

Wife definition of the problem: Husband hogs most of the money, and he doesn't love me anymore. How can I get more money from my husband? My husband needs to share more money with me. (underlying thoughts and feelings by wife: since Husband hogs most of the money, he doesn't love me anymore)(Husband giving her money meant he loved her)

After discussing, the wife who had felt unloved, found that her husband expressed his love by always wanting to provide for her, even in an emergency. He was loving her through saving for her.

Solution – Work on ways that husband could better express and show his love for his wife. She needed to be validated after many years of marriage, that he still loved and desired her. He also might want to give her a little more money.

The point is to make sure that the problem that you are trying to solve is really the problem.

Principle 7: Problem Solving: Brainstorming Possible Solutions

The goal of problem solving is to come up with the best possible solution that will work for the couple.

• You and Your partner should be clear on exactly what the problem is by now, and have clearly stated what the problem is.

• Brainstorming involves writing down all possible solutions thought of, not selecting anything at that point, but just naming the possibilities. After looking at the problem, and discussing the problem, start to brainstorm the possible alternatives, solutions, and outcomes. After looking at all the possible outcomes, the pros and cons, and who it will affect, decide together the best possible options and then pray for God to confirm is that a good solution or not. Both partners should have peace about the solution.

• There must be some give-and-take from both sides.

• Stick to one issue at a time, and after that issue is resolved, then move on to the next issue.

Things to Keep In Mind:

Solutions should benefit everyone involved. Solutions should not violate your conscious or be immoral. They should not violate the rights of others. They should be wholesome, pure, and lovingly motivated.

Principle 8: Negotiate Until An Agreement Is Reached

Disclaimer: Moral absolutes can never be negotiated, nor should. A wife should never negotiate with a husband about allowing him or her to do ungodly things. When we speak of negotiating it is in relation to things that are neutral and negotiable. Sinful behavior, morals, things of conscious can never be negotiated. Some things are non-negotiable.

After brainstorming and weighing the benefits, pros and cons, both partners will need to come to an agreement, on which path to take to solve their problem and implement the solution and then pray about it.

This seems pretty simple, right? Wrong. Often people have a hard time understanding the concept of negotiation. When negotiating, both have to see the others side and be willing and flexible to give their partner some of what they want and their partner give them some of what they want. This does not happen when people feel that they don't have to give up anything. Partners have to work on not being selfish or greedy. Selfishness and greed wants everything.

Principle 9: Give and Take

1 Corinthians 13:4 Charity suffereth long, and is kind; charity envieth not; charity vaunteth not itself, is not puffed up,

[5] Doth not behave itself unseemly, seeketh not her own, is not easily provoked, thinketh no evil;

[6] Rejoiceth not in iniquity, but rejoiceth in the truth;

[7] Beareth all things, believeth all things, hopeth all things, endureth all things.

[8] Charity never faileth: but whether there be prophecies, they shall fail; whether there be tongues, they shall cease; whether there be knowledge, it shall vanish away.

[9] For we know in part, and we prophesy in part.

Charity is the same as love. Remember love suffers long, is kind, does not envy, vaunts not, is not puffed up, does not behave unseemly, seeketh not her own, is not easily provoked, thinketh no evil, rejoiceth not in iniquity, but rejoiceth in truth, beareth all things, believeth all things, hopeth all things, endureth all things, and love never fails.

It always seeks the good of others.

Women seem to display these qualities more than men in relating to each other.

Women are usually the givers. Both partners should equally work on giving more and to take less. Our world would be a better transformed place if everyone gave and was not selfish.

Principle 10: Implementing the Solution

When both partners come to an agreement and they have prayed about the answer the solution should be implemented right away or as soon as it is feasible. There needs to be follow through. Couples must get into the habit of actually carrying out what they say they will do. Actions speak louder than words. The sooner the plan starts to get implemented, the sooner new habits are formed and can begin to be developed.

Principle 11: If Needs Be Agree to Disagree

If couples can't reach an agreement they must agree to disagree. Couples should be able to reach agreements on most issues. There are some problems, that they may not be able to reach an agreement on.   Did bought parties give the process their best? Were they honest and worked hard at problem solving? Did they fully understand the issues? Did they pray, read the Word, and asked the Holy Spirit? If so, and they still don't agree, work on solving the next problem, and revisit the issue at a later time. Continue to fast and pray about it.

Principle 12: If a Solution is Not Reached, The Wife Should Submit to Her Husband

If both partners can't agree or come to terms and agree on an issue, then agree to disagree. If both parties can't agree, then the wife should submit to her husband's wishes. This is the right thing to do because men are the leaders in the home and wives should follow their leadership; this is biblical.

God is the final authority.

Statistics

• Money and children (parenting) are what couples fight about the most; followed by sex, activities of partner (time spent doing other things), expectations (unmet needs, household chores, etc.), friends, and family.

• How a couple communicates is the biggest predictor of divorce.

• Couples that live together before marriage are more likely to get a divorce, than those that don't.

• Conflict that is not dealt with in marriage, affects marriage and children negatively.

• The divorce rate is about 50% in the U.S.

• Divorce in first marriages usually happens within the first 3 to 5 years.

- No fault laws have increased the rate of divorce.

More Statistics

Top Predictors of Marital Satisfaction

- Ability To Solve Problems Together

- Good communication

- Having realistic expectations

- Financially Responsible

- Religious

- Leisure Activities

- Mutual respect

- Similarities

- Love and affection

- Personality Compatibility

Understanding the Stages of Marriage

Understanding the different stages of a marriage, is important so that couples can plan how they will deal with the different stages as they occur. If couples understand what's coming they can more effectively deal with or plan for it.

The Stages of Marriage

Some stages of marriage have more conflict because of the season of life that couples are in, like when having children, because of changing roles and expectations, being new.

Honeymoon or Romantic Stage - This is the excitement stage of a relationship, usually lasting the first couple of years of meeting or of marriage. Everything about the other person is new and fresh, filled with fun and romance. There seems to be not a care in the world. Both persons are on cloud nine. Couples at this point, are wild, and hopeful with expectations, and often see their partner as perfect, or the way that they imagine or fantasize, rather than the way they really are. It is a period of discovery of the other person and adventure.

During this stage, there is usually not a lot of conflict, by the nature of the stage that the couples are in and all the excitement they are experiencing.

Reality Stage - In this stage of the relationship, the reality of the relationship has started to sink in a bit. Couples are still excited about their partner, but are getting to know them better, as they live together. What they thought of the other person, may not necessarily be true or still can be true, but the more human and real picture of their partner is beginning to be realized. At this point, they may realize they actually do disagree on some issues, as the real issues of life emerge.

Couples must understand as differences develop, during this stage, this is normal, and a part of getting to know someone better. The relationship transitions from fantasy to reality as a more real, normal, routine develops.

Having Children/Starting a Family Stage - This is the stage of life, when a couple begins to have children. In this stage of marriage, the marriage begins to shift to a focus on the children, as a primary responsibility. When the children are real young and during their adolescent years, it can be particularly stressful, because of new and changing roles and expectations that have emerged. This can put a strain on the marital relationship. The wife might feel tired, and don't want to have sex, etc. During these years, some conflict might be inevitable. There is a lot going on. Children demand a lot of the couple's time, along with work, and other commitments. There are financial obligations and maybe a need for a bigger home, etc.

Focusing on the marital relationship oftentimes becomes secondary, to the children, and the couple begins to operate as a family unit instead of a couple. During this period, feelings of intimacy have to be worked at, because the cares of life can be overwhelming and drain romance that is needed and crucial in all relationships.

During this period, the fantasy is over. The reality of dealing with all these new things gives a reality check real quick.

Accommodation Stage - During this stage, both persons are working at their marriage, understanding each other in a more real way, and better understanding their differences, and learning how to deal with conflict and differences. They are figuring out each other and themselves and what it is they really want and need. This stage is a little tricky, because at this stage a lot of marriages end. Couples who don't have a strong foundation in the Word of God, may be tired of their relationship, the kids are grown and gone, and they may be even searching for their purpose. Stand on God's and what God desires and he can give peace, love, and joy so that you live a Godly life.

Success Stage - During this stage of marriage, couples have been together for many years and have worked through a lot of issues and have come to terms with their partner. They have figured out what their partner wants and what they need. They have figured out what works and

continue to work at improving their marriage.

Closing Remarks

I hope this book has been helpful. To contact Connie Woods with any questions or comments, please email: conniewoods@comcast.net.

Other books by Connie Woods can be ordered on www.Amazon.com or from any bookstore by ISBN-13:9780692295854

- Living In the End Times: Matthew 24
- How to Be A Christian: The Romans Road to Salvation
- Spiritual Preparedness: 7 Things You Can Do To Prepare Yourself Spiritually
- Making Marriage Work: 12 Principles of Resolving Issues and Increasing Marital

Satisfaction and Intimacy & Building Long Lasting

Intimate Marriage

• 2014 Practical Guide For Christian Therapists &

Counselors

www.ingramcontent.com/pod-product-compliance
Lightning Source LLC
Chambersburg PA
CBHW031519040426
42445CB00009B/304